Forgiveness

Biblical Truth Simply Explained

Forgiveness

John Arnott

Chosen Books
A Division of Baker Book House Co
Grand Rapids, Michigan 49516

© 1997, 2003 by John Arnott

Published in the USA in 2003 by Chosen Books
a division of Baker Book House Company
P.O. Box 6287, Grand Rapids, MI 49516-6287
www.bakerbooks.com

Originally published under the title *What Christians Should Know About
... The Importance of Forgiveness* by Sovereign World Limited of
Tonbridge, Kent, England

Printed in the United States of America

Library of Congress Cataloging-in-Publication Data
Arnott, John (John G.)
    Forgiveness / John Arnott.
       p. cm. — (Biblical truth simply explained)
    Originally published: The importance of forgiveness. Tonbridge :
Sovereign World, c1997.
    ISBN 0-8007-9353-6
    1. Forgiveness—Religious aspects—Christianity. 2. Forgiveness—
Biblical teaching. I. Title. II. Series.

BV4647.F55A78 2003
234'.5—dc21

                                                        2003055057

Notes for study leaders

This book is a practical study of forgiveness and the importance of thinking and speaking positive words of life.

There are five study questions at the end of each chapter, designed to stimulate thought and challenge each person about his or her own attitudes about forgiveness. Praying together, asking for God's help, will help you all to take hold of the truths presented. This teaching is not just meant to be discussed—it is to be acted on, here and now.

As a leader, you will need to balance the needs of individuals with those of the whole group. Don't be surprised if different opinions and feelings arise during the study, particularly when answering certain questions. It is wise not to get sidetracked into devoting too much time to any one person's thoughts, but to enable everyone in the group to share and to respond to the positive message of the book.

It will help if the study takes place in an encouraging and receptive atmosphere where group members feel able to share openly. Encourage group members to read one chapter prior to each meeting and think about the issues in advance. Reviewing the content of the particular chapter at the meeting will refresh everyone's memory and avoid embarrassing those who have not managed to "do the homework."

Our hope is that as readers think and pray through the subject of forgiveness, they will fully forgive and be forgiven so that they can be more fruitful in all areas of their lives. May God bless you as you study this material yourself and lead others in doing so.

Contents

1

Words That Speak Life

The message of this book is that forgiveness is a key to blessing. Forgiveness and repentance open up our hearts and allow the river of God to flow freely in us.

We need to give the Holy Spirit permission to bring to our minds those things that need to be resolved in our hearts. Three things are vital to seeing a powerful release of the Spirit of God in our own lives and in the world around us.

First, we need a revelation of how big God is. We must know that absolutely nothing is impossible for Him, as the angel Gabriel said to Mary (Luke 1:37).

Second, we need a revelation of how loving and caring He is. I delight to tell people that God loves them just the way they are, yet loves them too much to leave them the way they are. He is absolutely committed to loving us into life.

As the Lord declares in Jeremiah 31:3–4,

> I have loved you with an everlasting love;
>   I have drawn you with loving-kindness.
> I will build you up again
>   and you will be rebuilt, O Virgin Israel.

Third, we need a revelation of how we can walk in that love and give it away. A heart that is free has resources available for others.

Energy-draining wounds

I have been a pastor for over twenty years. One thing I have discovered is that wounds in people's lives sap much of their energy and resources.

Many people expend so much energy on simply trying to make it through another day that they are unable to live a truly abundant life. They miss out on much of what God has for them, and there is little left over to give away to others.

When we ask people to have faith for things like missions, giving offerings or receiving miracles, many say, "I can hardly see my way clear to reach tomorrow, let alone think about this other stuff." They are unable to really go for God with abandonment. The answer is often locked up in the whole issue of repentance and forgiveness.

We don't get ensnared so much with people we are not close to, such as the man down the street or the woman in the next town. People we don't have close relationships with don't usually hurt us or anger us deeply.

The ones who can upset us are those we are close to—husbands, wives, parents, primary authority figures, pastors, teachers, employers, friends and those we have high expectations of. These people have the potential to hurt us. And when we are hurt, we can get into a pattern of thinking wrong and judgmental thoughts about them.

Constrained by the love of God

When He was asked what the greatest commandment is, Jesus said, "'Love the Lord your God with all your heart and with all your soul and with all your mind.' This is the first and greatest commandment. And the second is like it: 'Love your neighbor as yourself.' All the Law and the Prophets hang on these two commandments" (Matthew 22:37–40).

Many prophetic words are now going forth regarding mission and evangelism. The first missionaries went out because they were scattered by persecution. But I believe the Lord told me that the missionaries and evangelists He is sending now are going because they are hooked by the absolute love of God.

It is God's love that is constraining us and drawing us. When we go out loving and serving with pure, right motives, we will see this great harvest come in, the harvest of the end times. This is a demanding mandate from the Lord, and we cannot fulfill it if our energy is used in keeping a lid on personal problems and issues.

Critical thoughts and words

Negative things in our lives can block us from going out in love to serve others. Our thoughts, attitudes and words can all hinder us from moving freely in the grace of Christ.

Paul spoke of the need to conform our thoughts to those of Christ: "The weapons we fight with are not the weapons of the world. On the contrary, they have divine power to demolish strongholds. We demolish arguments and every pretension that sets itself up against the knowledge of God, and we take captive every thought to make it obedient to Christ" (2 Corinthians 10:4–5). Do you see how ungodly words actually set themselves up against God? Yet every thought and every aspect of our conversations must be obedient to Christ. If we want to bring our thoughts into subjection to Christ, we need to get free of the hold the enemy has on our lives. And the Lord has given us divine power to accomplish this.

Some years ago our church offered a course called *Pure in Heart,* written by Mark Virkler from Buffalo, New York. This course, now called *Counseled by God,* was worth a million dollars to me. It moved the issues of life from the theoretical and theological right down into the heart.

I will never forget the chapter on discerning the accuser (the devil) from the Comforter (God's Holy Spirit). In this chapter Mark made the outrageous statement that every negative thing and thought is always of the enemy, and every positive, life-giving, up-building thought is always of the Holy Spirit. He said that the enemy is always negative and the Holy Spirit is always positive.

That sounded extreme to me at first. I had to process and cross-examine that for several weeks before I finally agreed it was true. I concluded that even when God brings correction, it is always in a positive direction, and His intent is always life-giving and redemptive. Jesus said, "I have come that they may have life, and have it to the full" (John 10:10). That is His heart. The enemy, on the other hand, is always negative. "The thief comes only to steal and kill and destroy" (John 10:10). He is the accuser, the thief, the destroyer. His intent is to bring guilt, fear, hopelessness, sin and, ultimately, death. Mark pointed out that the accuser accuses, while the Comforter comforts. It's simple yet profound.

Since I was just learning in those days how to hear the voice of the Lord, I didn't realize that God would often speak in our thoughts. I thought that if we were diligent in prayer, then maybe once in a long while we might hear His voice in a spectacular way. The curtains would blow around, thunder would crash and we would say, "God spoke to me today."

I didn't realize that God speaks through ordinary thoughts. It had never occurred to me that there was and is a still, small voice behind me saying, "This is the way; walk in it" (Isaiah 30:21). And by the same token, we can also hear the devil's words being whispered in our ears.

Mark Virkler had discovered that even though he was a believer, approximately eighty percent of his thinking was critical, negative and accusatory, and only twenty percent was positive. To reinforce these statistics, the course included little quizzes about the way we think and speak. Not only were the others taking the class eighty percent negative and critical, but I was, too!

This smote me in my heart. I prayed, "God, this is completely unacceptable! I cannot go through my life with most of my mind yielded to the enemy!"

Whether you listen in on conversations of worldly people or of Christians, you find that others have the same problem. People talk about injustices against them. They rehearse what other people have done to them and go on about how they have been hurt. They rationalize why they are innocent victims of others' mistreatment.

Virkler says,

> Our enemy is subtle, using even instruments of righteousness for his wicked ends.... He may try to focus our attention on the laws of God and our total inability to keep them, rather than on the resurrection power of Jesus Christ within us which provides all the overcoming power necessary. He will encourage us to use Scripture to condemn and tear one another down, rather than for edification and encouragement as it is intended (Romans 15:4). We will find ourselves wielding the Bible as a club to judge and belittle rather than an instrument to bring hope and sanctification.[1]

So we are in this predicament where most of the time our thoughts are yielded to negative and judgmental thinking—thoughts that are really of the enemy. And we wonder why in the world we are not enjoying more of the blessings of God!

I remember responding, "Oh God, I don't want to be like this. You know I need You to help me with this

[1] Quoted from Mark Virkler's seminar "Counseled by God" from the Christian Leadership University teaching curriculum, www.cluonline.com. Used by permission.

one. I need You to give me a jab every time my mind starts to be negative and critical about people." I knew that in myself I didn't have the resources and self-discipline to get on top of it. I was afraid to simply promise God that I would stop. Only a miracle would transform my heart and thinking so that my thoughts could be positive and life-giving.

Remember the saying, "It is better to light one little candle than it is to curse the darkness"? We must desire to change. My prayer is, "Lord, I would like the numbers to be completely reversed. At the very least, help me to be only twenty percent negative and eighty percent positive." That would be more like it. How about you?

The power of the tongue

James chapter 3 reminds us that the tongue has great power for good or evil. Small things can have huge influence—as we know, a ship can be steered with a tiny rudder. Our out-of-control tongues can be like deadly poison when we say things that are to some degree irreparable. People have been deeply wounded by words spoken against them. I pray, "O God, O God, put a guard over my mouth. Put a guard over my thoughts. I don't want to wound and offend."

I don't want the Holy Spirit to have these kinds of issues with me. One of the most grievous things to the heart of God is all the criticism that goes on in the lives of Christians. Nothing stops revival like criticism!

Mark Virkler reminds us that there is often some

truth mixed in with the devil's messages. He says, "He is not so foolish as to expect you to accept outright lies. Instead he will mix truth with error in order to make it believable. May I suggest the following approximate equation: 85% truth + 15% error + destructive intent = satanic accusation."[2] What we listen to and what we say must not only be full of truth, but intended for good, not evil.

Jesus said, "The words I have spoken to you are spirit and they are life" (John 6:63). God is calling us into a place of victory where mercy triumphs over judgment. May our thoughts and conversations reflect that.

Choosing to speak life

In May 1996 I was with Pastor John Kilpatrick of the Brownsville Assembly of God in Pensacola, Florida. He described how years ago he had spent much time in prayer over his church's need for music ministry. He had often prayed, "O God, I want an orchestra."

He would walk through the empty orchestra area, where there was nobody to play any instruments, only the piano. Day after day he would complain about the emptiness. He would ask the Lord where the people were. "What is wrong with the Body of Christ? Why don't they serve? Why don't they get in here and play?" His words of judgment and condemnation were actually a curse on the church's music ministry.

One day the Lord spoke to him, "John, why don't you bless them instead?" The concept shocked him,

[2] Virkler, "Counseled by God." Used by permission.

but he began to walk through the place and say, "Lord, I bless this whole orchestra pit. I bless the people you are going to send. Lord, let the favor of God come upon them. I bless their hearts to want to play and worship and serve the King of Kings and the Lord of Lords."

It wasn't too long before someone came to him and said, "You know, I have a trumpet, and I used to play a little bit. I'm not all that good, but I'd like to play along with the piano, if that's all right." John was taken aback, but he said, "Great! Come on." And the next thing he knew, they came one after another. The whole orchestra area filled up with musicians.

Most importantly, God taught John the value of blessing and speaking words of life. The rest is history with the mighty revival that has happened at his church.

It is so important to speak life and not death.

Study questions:

1. How do wounds in people's lives sap their energy and resources?
2. How do we discern the enemy's voice from God's voice?
3. Give evidence of the way the Holy Spirit is edifying and upbuilding and the devil is destructive.
4. In what way does the tongue have tremendous power for good or evil?
5. How much of your own thinking and speech is negative, and how much is positive? Is it possible for you to change the ratio?

2

Mercy
Triumphs over Judgment

The trees of life and judgment

In Genesis 3 we find the story of two unique trees in the Garden of Eden. Rick Joyner has written about them, and so has Ted Haggard in his book *Primary Purpose*. I have taught about them for years, because I believe they are very important.

In the Garden grew two trees: the tree of life and the tree of the knowledge of good and evil. Which one did Adam and Eve eat of? Of course, they chose the forbidden tree of the knowledge of good and evil. They were tempted, wanting to be like God, knowing everything.

We could call this tree "the tree of judgment." In our pride and self-sufficiency we think we have enough understanding and information to make fair and honest judgments in every situation. We instinctively judge most of the time, and when we judge, we are usually negative, biased and unfair.

I believe the Holy Spirit is calling us to turn away from judging. We need to refrain from judging situations and judging one another, and instead bless and forgive so that life will flow.

Ted Haggard states that when we partake of the tree of the knowledge of good and evil, that is, the tree of judgment, it always produces accusation. When we accuse, we come into agreement with Satan, the accuser of the brethren. And whether it is someone else's fault or your own fault, somebody is always to blame when accusations fly.

That is the human condition. Our constant judging of others causes us to be negative, negative, negative.

Now that you and I have been born again and filled with the Holy Spirit, the tree of life has been put back into the gardens of our hearts. If we eat of the tree of life, what will happen? It will build us up, edify us and encourage us and others. The tree of life will give life to others as we bless and not curse, as we forgive and not accuse.

Ted Haggard declares that partaking of the tree of life—allowing the Holy Spirit to fill us and flow through us, and blessing and forgiving those around us—will always produce innocence. Where there is no accusation, there is no guilt.

Adam and Eve were innocent in the Garden before they ate of the tree of the knowledge of good and evil. Haggard notes that the anointing of the Holy Spirit will only flow through innocence.

The law of judgment

The Holy Spirit desires to search and work deep in our hearts.

> Do not judge, or you too will be judged. For in the same way as you judge others, you will be judged, and with the measure you use, it will be measured to you.
>
> Matthew 7:1–2

Do you believe those words? Jesus said it, I believe it and that settles it, right? Jesus is saying that if you demand justice and repayment for wrongs done to you, then you will be dealt with according to your own prescription. The way you treat people is the way you will be treated.

> Why do you look at the speck of sawdust in your brother's eye and pay no attention to the plank in your own eye? How can you say to your brother, "Let me take the speck out of your eye," when all the time there is a plank in your own eye? You hypocrite, first take the plank out of your own eye, and then you will see clearly to remove the speck from your brother's eye.
>
> Matthew 7:3–5

It seems that we have X-ray vision to see the short-comings of others, yet we seem quite blind to our own. Understanding this is a major key to freedom. Jesus is saying that you need to judge yourself first. When you want mercy for your own sins, then you tend to go much easier on others. Begin to bless and not curse. It will bring you tremendous release.

We can expend much energy in keeping our anger, fear and hurt pushed down. We are often not even in touch with those things in ourselves. But as we live in mercy and grace, releasing and forgiving others from these issues, we will find His yoke is easy and His burden is light (Matthew 11:30).

Justice is good, but mercy is better

When I understood this dynamic, I prayed, "Lord, I want to be the most forgiving, loving and understanding person on the face of the earth. I don't want to get what I deserve—not from You, not from Satan and not from life."

The Lord spoke to me years ago about this principle in Scripture: Justice is good, but mercy is better. Justice is the law of God. It means that if you hurt me, I can hurt you. If you wrong someone, then that wrong must be made right. Our sense of justice understands this. An eye for an eye, a tooth for a tooth, a life for a life—it's all very, very fair.

If you want justice, then you will be dealt with by the same rules. The law of God is good and fair, but it is also the arena in which Satan makes an appearance. He is the master prosecutor, the master accuser. James says, "Speak and act as those who are going to be judged by the law that gives freedom, because judgment without mercy will be shown to anyone who has not been merciful. Mercy triumphs over judgment!" (James 2:12–13). The problem is that none of us could ever have any hope for eternity if we all received the justice we deserved. There is, however, a place to go where Satan cannot follow and accuse. That place is the grace of the Lord Jesus Christ. It is a place of mercy, love and forgiveness. This is a higher and better place. If we live in grace and mercy, Satan cannot follow us there, because he has no rights there. Did you know that if you spend eighty percent of your time on the level of judgment and justice, then the enemy has the right to beat you eighty percent of the time? My cry is, "God, help me to live more in the grace of God."

The law of sowing and reaping

Let's hear the words of our Lord: "Do not judge, and you will not be judged. Do not condemn, and you will not be condemned. Forgive, and you will be forgiven. Give, and it will be given to you. A good measure, pressed down, shaken together and running over, will be poured into your lap. For with the measure you use, it will be measured to you" (Luke 6:37–38). Isn't it amazing how often we view this sowing and reaping only in terms of financial giving? Yet this dynamic applies across the board. It is for releasing the incredible grace of God. However, this sowing and reaping can also be for evil.

In Exodus 20:5 we are told that the sins of the fathers are visited upon the children to the third and fourth generation. As we see recurring patterns of negative things happening to us, we can also see how the enemy has had inroads into our lives. He wants to maintain this access right down through the family line for several generations.

Consider, for example, an alcoholic father who has an alcoholic son who in turn has an alcoholic son. Or a young woman who grows up in an abusive home and vows that she will never marry a man who is abusive. Five years after the wedding, she is saying, "I can't stand living with him anymore. He is beating me and being cruel to the children. He is just like my father." Meanwhile, we think, "What is wrong with these people? Couldn't they see this coming?"

There is an incredible magnetic pull that causes people to play into the hands of the enemy. We see this with hereditary sins, especially addictive and compulsive behavior. Satan is a master legalist, taking advantage of the law of sowing and reaping (Galatians 6:7–8) for his own purposes.

So people make judgments toward their parents that give the enemy legal right to perpetuate the crime. Yet the heart of God is to forgive and heal.

Justice or mercy?

Jesus took what we rightly deserve upon Himself, on the cross. When we say, "I hate my father and never want to see him again; he deserves all he gets," rightly accusing him and blaming him for things he has done and said, we are making a judgment that is rooted in hurt and bitterness. We are also demanding justice, which means that we are actually stepping back into a legal system that has power to demand justice and payment for our own sins as well.

The only safe response is, "Lord, let there be mercy.

Let mercy triumph over judgment. You have forgiven me all this great debt of mine. Now that You have given me the keys to the Kingdom, I am going to forgive everybody who owes me anything or has hurt me in any way."

Remember Matthew 18:23–35, in which Jesus told the story about the king who loaned money to one of his servants. The man ran up a huge debt—the equivalent of millions of dollars.

One day the king called him in and demanded, "Pay back what you owe me." The man said, "I can't. Have mercy on me and give me time, and I will pay you back everything." But the king said, "No, I want it now. Sell him. Sell his family. Liquidate everything he has. We will recover as much as we can."

So the man fell down and begged for forgiveness, saying, "Please have mercy upon me." Then the king said, "Okay, you'll never be able to pay the debt back anyway, so forget it. Just go on about your business. I release you from your debt." How relieved and thankful that man must have been.

However, Jesus describes how, soon after that, that same man went out and took another servant by the neck, saying, "Pay me the fifty dollars you owe me!" His fellow servant replied with the same plea: "Have mercy on me. Give me time, and I will pay all of it back to you." But the first man said, "No way!" and had him thrown into jail before the debt was paid.

The word got back to the king. He called the man in and said, "You wicked servant. I had compassion and mercy upon you for this huge debt that you owed me.

Could you not have had mercy upon your fellow servant?"

Even though I knew that story, I was tempted to rationalize that I didn't sin so badly compared to everybody else. A dualism was going on in my heart—I wanted mercy for myself but justice in my dealings with others. "They hurt me, they said this, they did that, they owe me and I want it put right." But for myself I wanted grace and mercy.

We can't have it both ways. If I am going to say I want justice because someone hurt me, then I cannot ask for mercy for myself. That is what the wicked manager did. But if I try to exact justice, I have fallen from the place of grace and mercy, back to what is "fair."

The truth is that people hurt people. Parents hurt their children. Children hurt their parents. Many people have been hurt by their pastors. Many pastors have been hurt by their people. This is happening all over the Body of Christ.

When we ask people about their parents, their sisters and brothers and their childhood experiences, we often find years of baggage and judgments that people, for the most part, are not in touch with. Then they wonder why there are recurring patterns of pain and rejection in their lives.

The place of mercy

Why not come to the place where we say, "Lord, I forgive everybody of everything"? We can then let go of our claims for justice and repayment. The injustices are laid at the cross, and the mercy and grace of Christ can then flow into our lives. Love then covers a multitude of sins (1 Peter 4:8).

The Kingdom of God is not about keeping religious rules and regulations; it is about righteousness, peace and joy in the Holy Spirit (Romans 14:17), which pleases God and even receives human approval (Romans 4:18). That joy is something that you and I have as we live and remain in the place of mercy.

Study questions:

1. Explain the significance of the two trees in the Garden of Eden.
2. Why is mercy better than justice?
3. How does Satan take advantage of the law of sowing and reaping?
4. What does Matthew 18:23–35 tell us about our desire for mercy for ourselves but judgment for others? What does it say about God's order of things?
5. What happens when we lay down our claims for justice and repayment? Are you prepared to do this yourself?

3

Choosing to Forgive

In these days God is blessing us so abundantly. I see many people forgiving each other and repenting before one another. As they do, they are released into great freedom—freedom to fulfill their destiny in God's Kingdom.

Freed through forgiveness

Carol and I started our first church in Stratford, Ontario, Carol's small hometown where most people know each other. We were the new kids in town and were called a "cult" and various other names by some of the other churches.

About twelve years later, I had the privilege of being asked to talk to a group of pastors near Toronto at one of their district meetings. A pastor came up to me and said, "John, I need to ask your forgiveness, because I was so wrong. I thought we had some kind of a corner on the Kingdom of God. I believed that if something wasn't happening with us, it just wasn't happening. I am so sorry, and I want to ask your forgiveness."

This man was formerly the pastor of a church in Stratford who had denounced us from his pulpit. When I related this to a former member of his church, who was now with us in Toronto, he broke down and wept as the Lord poured His healing into that situation.

Recently a pastor from one of the largest churches in Toronto made an appointment to see me. He said, "John, I've come to ask your forgiveness." I asked him why, and he said, "I have said nasty, terrible things about you and about your church, and more importantly, about this move of the Spirit."

He told me that when I had originally phoned him, inviting him to our church because God was visiting us, he had reacted negatively and didn't want anything to do with us. He had denounced the move of God over and over again. Later he heard about revival in Pensacola, Florida, and he traveled all the way there to experience it. God so touched his heart and convicted him that he had to come see me.

He was so moved that he also came to our Sunday morning service and asked the congregation's forgiveness for speaking against them and the move of God. He confided, "John, we so desperately need revival. I know I have grieved the Holy Spirit by criticizing you, and I don't want any outstanding debts in the heavenly places. I don't want God to have anything against me. I want revival for my soul and revival for my church. I want God's blessing to open up." Needless to say, a great healing came between our two churches.

Do you wonder why situations like this are being healed? God is calling His whole Church into this place of repentance and forgiveness. The heavens are being torn open because people are finding out that mercy triumphs over judgment. They are willing to do what Jesus said: forgive one another, give grace to one another and love one another. We want to see forgiveness flowing for individuals, families, churches, cities and nations.

Our debt to Jesus Christ

Think about the greatest crime that ever occurred among humanity. It was not Hitler, Stalin or any other despot guilty of murdering millions of people. The greatest atrocity of all was when our ancestors, Jews and Romans, murdered the Son of God on a rough cross two thousand years ago.

Consider who Jesus really was. He was not just a good man and wise teacher. He was God the Son, who came to earth, where He healed, spoke truth, blessed, gave and shared of Himself. Wicked hands nailed Him to a cross, mocking Him while he bled to death. He endured it because there had to be an atoning payment for our sins, and the innocent paid the debts of the guilty.

It is your debt and mine that He has paid. It was our sin—yours and mine—that necessitated His execution. We are responsible for the terrible death of God's Son. Our sins required His death, and we are the spiritual children of those who murdered Him.

To that debt, we have piled on our own lives of immorality, our secret pornographic sins and adulterous relationships, our stealing and lying and killing and backbiting. We have added our slander and accusations and our own bitter judgments against ourselves and others.

So we had a huge, accumulated debt. Then we came to Jesus saying, "Lord, I want to settle this thing out of court. I don't want to wait until Judgment Day and get what I deserve. I owe you a great debt, and I am unable to pay you. Will you please have mercy on me and forgive me?" And He said, "My child, step up into the grace and mercy of the Lord Jesus Christ. My Son took your place; your debt is cleared."

Such sweet forgiveness came. It was just as though we had never sinned. All the wrong we had done was completely covered. Jesus died instead of us and paid off every debt that you and I would ever owe.

This was the greatest overpayment in the history of the universe. The Son of God traded His perfect and innocent life for the guilty. God himself paid off what you owe and what I owe. No one just makes it into heaven: We are either in by a mile or miss it by a mile.

God then says, "Now, if you want to live in this place where you receive My full forgiveness, you must be forgiving." That is the deal. In other words, I cannot ask for mercy for me and justice for you. It is all or nothing. It is mercy without justice or justice without mercy. Can you see that clearly? You can have mercy or you can have justice, but you can't have both.

Choose to forgive

> Our Father in heaven,
> hallowed be your name,
> your kingdom come,
> your will be done on earth as it is in heaven.
> Give us today our daily bread.
> Forgive us our debts, *as we also have forgiven* our
>   debtors.
> And lead us not into temptation,
> but deliver us from the evil one.
>
> Matthew 6:9–13, emphasis added

Have you noticed that in there before? We are forgiven "as we also have forgiven." The same way we forgive, the Lord forgives us.

Notice particularly what Jesus goes on to say: "For if you forgive men when they sin against you, your heavenly Father will also forgive you. But if you do not forgive men their sins, your Father will not forgive your sins" (Matthew 6:14–15). The choice is clear: mercy or justice. Which would you prefer?

Now, before you get paranoid and fearful, keep in mind that the grace of God has been given to help you live this out. I believe very much that it is a process. But so much hurt, fear and pain has come upon the Body of Christ that it makes the process difficult. Sometimes the pain is so severe or the wrong so outrageous that we feel entitled to hold on to our hurt and anger.

The trap of self-justification

Matthew 5:23–24 tells us that when we come and bring our gifts before the Lord, and there we remember that our brother or sister has something against us, we should first go and be reconciled with him or her and then return and offer our gifts. Then we will have clean hearts.

In Luke 18 Jesus tells us about the Pharisee and the publican (or tax collector). The Pharisee said, "Thank you, Lord, that I am not like that other man. I fast and pray and tithe. I do all these good things for you" (verses 11–12, author's paraphrase).

The tax collector came in abject humility and prayed, "God, have mercy on me, a sinner" (verse 13), not comparing himself to anyone else, just admitting how guilty and in need of God's mercy he was. Jesus said that the man who came in humility went away justified, but the self-righteous one did not.

Let me bring this down to a practical level. I was in Winnipeg, Canada, preaching on the grace of God and the power of forgiveness. A man came up to me after the service, shaking and very troubled. He said, "John, you don't understand what has happened to me." I listened as he told his story.

He said, "My own father severely abused my three-year-old baby girl. A government agency became involved, and it has devastated our family. Our little girl has nightmares all the time. Furthermore, my father denies it. My whole family is angry at me. It is an absolute catastrophe, and now you are telling me I have to forgive him."

I said, "Sir, I am not telling you that you have to forgive him. I am telling you that the only way out of your prison is forgiveness, and then repentance for judging. You can have justice if you want, but if you do, realize that the enemy will see to it that you also get what you deserve. If you can work through the issues and become willing to forgive, God will give you grace and help as you unravel all this pain. Then you can remain in the place of His mercy."

Some people have been the victims of unbelievable tragedies. They know that they have been wronged, but they don't understand that their own recurring problems have anything to do with their sins of judging. Their own self-justification is too beguiling.

Our free will

When people sin, other people usually get hurt. It's not fair, is it? We may ask why God allows it. It's because He has given us free will to make right choices or wrong choices. We may choose to love, or we may choose to sin.

Free will is fundamental to love. In order to have love flowing, people must be free to choose. They may choose to be near one another and bless one another, but it is of their own free will. Otherwise, we would just be robots.

So we can choose to bless or we can choose to hurt, to be selfish. We can give life, or we can give death. That choice is the responsibility that goes along with free will. Every time people make a wrong choice or do something outside of love, it injures either them or someone else—or both. Then we have what I like to call the "sinner" and the "sinned-against."

When we are the sinner, and the Holy Spirit reminds us of it, we want mercy, don't we? But when we are the sinned-against, we cry for justice and often become bitter. We don't realize this as a subtle trap of the enemy. If Satan can hook us through this, if he can get us demanding justice, then he will be legally entitled to bring into our lives all the reaping and punishment we deserve.

That is the enemy's plan. That is what gives him power and legal rights. Yet Jesus, against whom the greatest crime of all was committed, didn't say, "Father, get these murderers and give them what they deserve." The cry that came from his lips, even in that situation of extreme agony, was "Father, forgive them, for they do not know what they are doing" (Luke 23:34).

That is why Hebrews 12:24 says that the blood of Jesus speaks much better things than the blood of Abel. Abel's blood cried out, "God, avenge me. My brother has taken away my life" (see Genesis 4:10, author's paraphrase). Jesus' blood, however, cried out, "Forgive them, for they do not know what they are doing." Mercy triumphs over judgment.

Bringing judgment on ourselves

Recently a friend and I were discussing the fact that it is often difficult to see healing come to seasoned Christians. At the same time, it can be relatively easy to pray for non-Christians, and we see God heal them or do miracles.

You can pray for fellow employees at work or for a stranger on the street, and God will grant all kinds of miraculous answers to prayer for people who don't know Him or go to church. But some dear old saint who has been serving the Lord for years will have nothing happen when you pray healing for him or her. Why?

There are often issues needing forgiveness and repentance that remain unresolved through fear, pride, anger or pain. First Corinthians 11:27–29 gives us one key to this mystery: "Whoever eats the bread or drinks the cup of the Lord in an unworthy manner will be guilty of sinning against the body and blood of the Lord. A man ought to examine himself before he eats of the bread and drinks of the cup. For he who eats and drinks without recognizing the body of the Lord eats and drinks judgment on himself." I have read that passage for years, assuming that it was only referring to the Communion elements. But it is not only referring to the broken body of our Lord Jesus Christ. It also refers to His Body, the Church! We are His Bride, and His Body is precious to Him. It grieves Him deeply when we slander the Body of Christ by speaking against one another.

Paul continues, "That is why many among you are weak and sick, and a number of you have fallen asleep. But if we judged ourselves, we would not come under judgment. When we are judged by the Lord, we are being disciplined so that we will not be condemned with the world" (1 Corinthians 11:30–32). What a powerful word. If we will admit our own sins of judging everybody and everything and ask God to forgive us, we will not come under judgment.

The place of grace

The world welcomes justice. I, too, thank God for justice, for the police and the courts and for laws, but there is a higher and better place. There is a place where Satan cannot follow you, the place of the grace of the Lord Jesus Christ. This is what Christianity is all about. It is here that life and mercy flow, for us and others.

Do you know that when you live in grace you are invincible until God is finished with you? The enemy can't follow you there, because there is no grace for Satan—he is stuck with the law! But we can live in grace and be absolutely dependent on the Holy Spirit's ability to keep us.

Jesus is totally and absolutely victorious in all of these areas. He completely defeated Satan. Jesus is God, who came to us as a human being, but one empowered by the Holy Spirit. He said, "The one whom God has sent speaks the words of God, for God gives the Spirit without limit" (John 3:34).

Jesus had the Spirit without measure. He completely defeated Satan and all of the hordes of hell single-handedly. Nothing has changed—they are still defeated. Yet we give Satan power when we choose justice rather than mercy.

Somebody once told me that as a Christian I don't have rights anymore. This is absolutely true. The only rights we have are the rights to be totally forgiven as we forgive others, to go to heaven when we die, to be a love slave to the Lord Jesus Christ and to rely on Him for everything.

Study questions:

1. Explain "the greatest overpayment in the history of the universe."
2. Why must we choose between mercy and justice?
3. How does the blood of Christ speak much better things than the blood of Abel (Hebrews 12:24)?
4. How can self-justification and judgment of other Christians be a trap for us?
5. What is the place of grace? Are you living there?

4

Set Free from the Fruits of Judgment

(by Carol Arnott)

Hebrews 12:15 contains a very important message for the Church: "See to it that no one misses the grace of God and that no bitter root grows up to cause trouble and defile many." I would like to talk about how this verse applies to our lives, from the basis of my own testimony.

When I became a Christian, I learned about forgiveness. So I forgave my mother, who had hurt me deeply, for everything and anything, yet I found that I still didn't love her. I went through it all again, only to find that I still didn't love her. So again and again I went through the motions of forgiving, and still I didn't love her.

I thought, *God, there must be something wrong. What is wrong with my forgiveness?*

Judging born out of hurt

My mother was the last of eight children in a farming family, the sixth girl. The family was hoping for more

41

boys to work the farm, so my mom wasn't even wanted. She was just another girl.

Since my mother's parents often worked in the field, her sisters were expected to raise her. But kids being kids—and perhaps not very well mothered themselves—they were often very cruel to her. They would rock her violently in her cradle. When she cried as a little toddler, they would lock her in a closet.

You can imagine the wounds these events caused in her heart. But as a child growing up, I didn't understand my mother's pain and rejection. I didn't know the depths of her hurts. I just had to deal with how she was to me.

When kids do something wrong, when they are bad and really deserve a spanking, they know it. But when children are punished for things they didn't do, they are keenly aware of the injustice. They may not rebel outwardly, but in their hearts they judge their parents as cruel or unjust.

That's what happened to me. In my case, I was too afraid to rebel outwardly because I would be severely beaten. My mother would take my dad's belt and whack me—today it would be called physical abuse. I would be black and blue and have welts on my body, but the deeper marks were left on the inside. In my heart I hated her; inside I judged her and despised her.

When I became a Christian, I realized I had a lot of unforgiveness in my heart that needed to be released. I worked through all I could, but it didn't seem to change my feelings toward my mother. I thought, "God, there is something wrong here." Over and over I tried, but my heart was not changed. It wasn't until I received some teaching from John and Paula Sandford about judgments rooted in bitterness that I gained more understanding.

The Scripture says to honor your mother and your father only if they are good Christians and if they do everything right. Oops! It doesn't say that, does it?— even if we might want it to! No, it says, "Honor your father and your mother, as the LORD your God has commanded you, so that you may live long and that it may go well with you in the land the LORD your God is giving you" (Deuteronomy 5:16). Conversely, in the areas in which we dishonor our parents, it will not go well with us. We don't usually judge our parents in all areas, but we judge and dishonor them in areas where we have been hurt or neglected.

I thought, *Well, God, I don't understand. I have forgiven her. What is going on?* He told me, "You have not honored her. You have sinned by dishonoring your mother."

He began to show me that there were two sides to the issue. We need to forgive, yes, but we also need to repent of our own sin of judging. I had forgiven my mother, but on the other hand, I didn't honor her in my heart. I hated her and judged her.

That was my sin, not hers. My reaction to her was sinful, yet I didn't see that. Satan, being a legalist, went to God and said, "Carol has sinned here. She has not repented from this sin of judging her mother, so I have the legal right to bring the law of sowing and reaping into her life."

Reaping what I had sown

Have you ever kept a garden and planted seeds? If you've ever planted corn or maize, how many seeds (kernels) do you get back for every one you sow? Not one, but hundreds. The law of increase is that for every single seed you plant, you get many more. So through my judgments of a domineering, controlling mother, I reaped a harvest through other domineering and controlling women in my life.

I would get controlled and manipulated, used and hurt by these women, and I would never see the problems coming. When they did come, I would wonder what I did to bring it on. I asked God, "Have I got a sign on my back that says, 'Come on, control and dominate me?'"

Well, yes, I did have a sign. In the spirit realm I wore such a sign because I judged my mother. The law of sowing and reaping was being enforced by the enemy.

Eventually, I went to my mother. By this time she was a Christian, and I said, "Mom, I just received some teaching, and I realize that I have sinned against you. I have judged you. I have hated you in my heart, and I really want to work things through."

She said, "Carol, I don't want to talk about it. I am too old. Too much has happened. I don't want you ever to mention this to me again."

Disappointed, I wondered, "Now what am I going to do?"

God does the healing

The Lord asked me, "Carol, do you want to be healed?" I said, "Yes, Lord, I want to be healed." He said, "Give Me permission to dig in the garden of your heart. You don't need to go rooting around, turning everything up and being worried. I don't want you to start navel-gazing or to strive. Give Me permission to bring up the issues where you have judged and that need to be dealt with." I said, "All right. Lord, I give You permission."

Then I said a blanket prayer: "God, I realize that I have sinned by judging my mother and not honoring her. Lord, I forgive her for everything she has ever done to me. She owes me nothing. I ask for her forgiveness, and I give You permission to show me the areas I need to put right."

That prayer initiated a trek of three and a half years of major dealing with issues. The Lord would bring up ten, maybe fifteen, issues of judgment a day—things I had long forgotten about. I worked through situations I had not thought about since the day they happened.

I would pray, "Lord, I sinned by judging my mother. I forgive her for that incident. I did not honor her in it; instead, I judged and hated her. Lord, I forgive her. Please, Lord, forgive me for the sin of judging my mother." This happened without much feeling in my heart—nothing emotional really seemed to happen.

I would see my mother about twice a week or more,

and to the best of my ability I would try to love her. I would tell her I loved her and give her a hug. I did the best I was able to do.

About three years into the process, I was visiting my mother one day. When I was about to leave, I hugged her, told her I loved her and said good-bye. But this time a surprising and wonderful love for my mother welled up in my heart. I knew I was healed. I knew that God had done a work in my heart.

Do you know what else? Not only did God heal me, but when I released my mother it set her free, too. She is so much better, much freer and more loving. My healing allowed God to do mighty works in her life even though she wasn't able to work through the issues herself because of her pain and lack of knowledge and application of Scripture.

Giving Satan legal rights

In the first church where John and I were pastors, I had a problem. People would come up to me and complain to me, but never to John. They felt neglected or rejected and would dump all their negativity on me. When I told John how people were treating me, it seemed that he wouldn't or couldn't hear me.

If any of you have heard John speak about me, you know that he absolutely adores me. He loves me, and I know that if anyone tried to really hurt me, he would stand up for me. But when it came to the people in this church, he seemed unable to.

I would go to him and tell him what was said, and

sometimes he would say, "Oh, you are just jealous," or "You are overreacting again," or "That is not all that serious." I would then feel devastated.

Then, when we started the church in Toronto, the same thing happened. The people there didn't go to John with their complaints either; they came to me. When I went to John, he wouldn't stand up for me. He wouldn't even take my side or hear what they were saying. This was driving me to distraction.

Finally, I cried out, "God, what on earth is going on? What am I reaping here?" And the Lord reminded me of my feelings about my father. I was shocked. "My father? My father is a wonderfully loving and kind man. He's a sweetheart, a gentleman. I love my father. I have no judgments against him."

The Lord said, "Oh yes, you do. You judged your father because he did not protect you from your mother."

Those judgments gave the enemy legal rights that resulted in the primary man in my life, John, not being able to protect me from "mother" church. The church then was able to dump all its rubbish on me. John was not able to stand up for me. The laws of judging, and of sowing and reaping, gave the enemy what he needed.

I thought, *Lord, could that really be possible?* I was still reasonably new to this kind of teaching. It sounded so strange. So I went to a friend and said, "I think this is what the Lord has been telling me. I want to confess it to you. I am not going to tell John. I am just going to forgive my father for not standing up for me and for not protecting me from my mother's wrath. I am going to release and forgive him, and then I am going to forgive John for not standing up for me, for not protecting me from the people in the church. I am going to ask the Lord to forgive me for judging my father and John."

I asked the Lord to put the cross of Jesus between my heart and the law of sowing and reaping, and I left it there.

Two months later there was another incident. A lady came to me and dumped a lot of nasty stuff on me. I went to John, and immediately he said, "We are going to call her into the office." He called her in, stood up for me and dealt with the situation. It was amazing. He has been the same way ever since.

My judgments had given Satan legal right to hold John in bondage and to prevent him from being my protector.

If there are areas in your life where repetitive, negative things keep happening, if there are areas where you are unable to love someone as you should, look back and say, "Holy Spirit, will you show me? Will you reveal it to me if I have judged a primary person in my life? Have I dishonored him or her?"

You may not be in touch with the anger, hurt or emotions. You may not have recollection of ever judging anyone, but if bad fruit keeps appearing in your life, there is usually a judgment rooted in bitterness, anger or hurt that is allowing the enemy access. Keep in mind that it will not be in every area of your life, but it will be in the areas where you have been hurt and wounded.

Set free

The Lord has come to set the captives free, to heal the brokenhearted and to open the prison doors (Isaiah 61:1). He has come to do that not only for me, but for all of us.

I believe the enemy has held us in bondage and kept much of the Body of Christ in darkness. All the time, the Lord has made available a way of release and forgiveness, but Satan tries to keep this truth hidden from the Body of Christ. The Bible says, "My people are destroyed from lack of knowledge" (Hosea 4:6).

In my own life this truth has meant more than any money could buy. It has meant healing and freedom. God has set me free! It is so gloriously liberating.

Study questions:
1. What are judgments rooted in hurt or bitterness?
2. How is repentance a vital part of forgiveness?
3. Explain how the law of increase works, when we reap what we sow.
4. How can we unwittingly give Satan legal rights to harm us through others?
5. Are there areas in your own life where repetitive, negative things keep happening? Are you committed to letting God set you free?

5

It's Time to Forgive

Now we can understand what Jesus meant when He said, "I will give you the keys of the kingdom of heaven; whatever you bind on earth will be bound in heaven, and whatever you loose on earth will be loosed in heaven" (Matthew 16:19).

It is time to take these keys away from the enemy. We must recognize where we have unresolved issues, outstanding IOUs that say "I owe you" or "You owe me." We need to uncover those judgments that are deeply rooted in pain and bitterness.

We need to realize where we are demanding God's justice instead of His mercy, and deal with these issues through forgiveness and repentance. Holding on to hurts and judgments is a luxury you and I can't afford.

The threshing floor

I believe that God is taking us prophetically to the place of the threshing floor. The Lord is breaking off that hard outer shell or husk and preparing us to become food for the nations. When the grain is separated from the chaff, then the wheat is ready to use.

People asked John the Baptist if he was the Messiah, and he answered them, "I baptize you with water. But one more powerful than I will come, the thongs of whose sandals I am not worthy to untie. He will baptize you with the Holy Spirit and with fire" (Luke 3:16). Many of us love these familiar verses and have heard many messages on receiving the Holy Spirit. But let's read the words that follow: "His winnowing fork is in his hand to clear his threshing floor and to gather the wheat into his barn, but he will burn up the chaff with unquenchable fire" (Luke 3:17). The Lord is telling us that He is committed to burning up the chaff in our lives. This is central to our relationship with Him. The Lord wants to knock the chaff off us and set us free, burning away the undesirable things so that we will, with a pure heart, flow in the grace, love and mercy of God.

Are we really willing to have Him do this? I believe this is a do-or-die season, a crisis time. Our lives will go one way or the other on the threshing floor. God will thoroughly purge His threshing floor.

Loosing others through forgiveness

We have been given a treasure. When we gave our lives to Jesus, we went from nothing to everything. We have been forgiven a huge debt of sin, and God is saying now, "The least you can do is to forgive your fellow servants, your parents, your brothers."

I know of women whose brothers literally tortured them as they were growing up. Things may also have happened to you that have caused you to hate men, or to hate women.

When my first marriage broke up, I made a vow in my heart that no woman would ever hurt me like that again. It took me quite a while, with Carol's help, to break down that vow. I thank God that Carol penetrated my defenses. It meant that I was able to be healed of judgments rooted in bitterness, and to see mercy triumphing over judgment.

Often the tragedies of life are so serious and so severe that we can't imagine letting go of them, especially with one simple prayer. Sometimes the wound is too fresh, and we need more time.

One of the reasons why the apostle Paul had such an outstanding conversion was because a man named Stephen, whom they were stoning to death, understood this principle and cried out, "Lord, do not hold this sin against them" (Acts 7:60).

Perhaps his eyes caught the eyes of young Saul of Tarsus at that moment. Because Stephen forgave, there was no binding in the heavens, no surrendering of keys and rights to the enemy so he would be able to legally hold Saul. God later powerfully intervened, and Saul was dramatically saved. Today we know him as Paul, the apostle to the Gentiles.

We are to give others a gift they don't deserve when there is no question that we have been sinned against, hurt and violated by them. Yes, an outstanding debt exists. They owe us, but we can give them an undeserved gift—our forgiveness. We can step into the mercy of God and say, "I want mercy to triumph over justice." This is what God is asking for.

The grace of the Lord Jesus Christ is enough for me. I am going to give a gift of forgiveness to those who have hurt me and sinned against me. I am going to give them a gift they don't deserve—my forgiveness—just as my heavenly Father has given me a gift that I don't deserve—His forgiveness.

I want mercy for myself, not the justice I deserve. Therefore, I choose to forgive others. It is the merciful who obtain mercy (Matthew 5:7).

Sometimes it takes a while, just as in Carol's story, to give the Holy Spirit permission to uncover the issues. But God wants to make us into free, happy and joy-filled people. We don't have to waste our time or energy keeping a lid on all of the hurt, anger and fear the enemy brings into our lives through the law of sowing and reaping.

Remember, Satan will move through legal rights. We need to give up our rights, surrendering and saying, "Lord, I want to do things Your way." We can be like Jesus and Stephen who said, "Lay not this sin to their charge." Let's tell God, "I forgive them, and I ask You to forgive me for judging them in bitterness and hurt, and for demanding that something be done about it."

Keep in mind that there are many situations where loving pastoral correction needs to be brought to bear. I am not speaking against this. I am talking about issues that are poisoning your heart, areas where you are literally giving Satan access to your life, enabling him to come and bring destruction any time he chooses.

There is a place of quiet rest near the heart of God. There is a place under the shadow of the Almighty. There is a place at the cross of Jesus Christ where mercy triumphs over judgment and you can come into the glorious liberty of the children of God. It is the place of grace.

I am not going to put a gun to your head and say you have to forgive! That doesn't work. Most of us have been told things like, "Well, I don't care what they did. If you are a Christian, you have to forgive!" Sometimes forced forgiveness is only partial; it buries the wound without real healing. You don't have to forgive. You can hold on to it if you like, but understand the dynamics.

You are entitled to justice, but then you will also reap what you have sown. You, too, will receive what you deserve instead of mercy. When I understood that, I knew what Jesus meant when He said, in Matthew 5:7, "Blessed are the merciful, for they will be shown mercy."

Let forgiveness flow

I believe that the Word of the Lord has penetrated your heart like a sword, and the Holy Spirit has you at the threshing floor where He wants to knock some of this chaff off your life. Are there a few people you need to forgive?

Let me lead you in a prayer. Please don't strive. You

may be thinking, "I can say the words, but I can't make myself really mean them." That is okay as long as in your heart you are saying, "Lord, help me to work through this. Make me willing to be willing." God honors that.

Also, we are going to ask God to forgive us for the sin of judging others and ask Him to graciously remind us when we lapse into thinking negatively again.

Let's bless and not curse. Let's give undeserved gifts to people so that we can be vessels of honor and mercy. Become a new wineskin that will hold the new wine and the oil of the Holy Spirit, enabling you to walk in freedom and love.

Before I lead you in this prayer, let's take a moment and wait upon God. Be bathed in the presence of the Holy Spirit. Invite Him to come upon you afresh. Don't strive to do this in religious strength or out of your willpower. Without the Holy Spirit's enabling, you won't be able to proceed.

Some of you have been terribly abused. The circumstances you have gone through and the things that have happened to you were never, never of the Father's heart. They were born from sin loosed in the world and from the people who have hurt you, as well as your own wrong choices. God is not responsible for human sin.

We can defeat the devil. We can make sure that the sins of the fathers are not passed on to the children to the third and fourth generation. For if you don't deal with your legalistic judgments and step into grace and mercy, the Bible says that the problems are passed on to your children (Exodus 20:5). The master legalist, Satan, will see to it.

Let's pray together:

We worship You, Father. We come to You, acknowledging our need. We ask for the presence of the Holy Spirit to come and help us. We choose mercy over judgment. We want to give gifts of forgiveness to those who hurt us and those who don't deserve it. We want to defeat the enemy and take away his legal rights to harm us.

Father, I choose to forgive the ones who have hurt me so deeply and sinned against me. I forgive my mother, and I forgive my father. I forgive my brothers. I forgive my sisters. I forgive my husband. I forgive my wife. I forgive my employers and my pastors and my friends and everyone who has sinned against me. I give them the gift of unconditional forgiveness, with no strings attached. They owe me nothing. I trust You to turn it for good.

Lord, I also forgive myself for my own failures and mistakes. I let go of it all.

Lord, now I want to confess my sins. I have judged these whom I have mentioned in bitterness and anger. I want to be free. Forgive me, Father, for dishonoring my parents, my pastor, my friends. Forgive me for becoming part of the problem rather than part of the solution. It was my own pride that was demanding justice. "Forgive us our debts, as we also have forgiven our debtors" [Matthew 6:12].

Lord, I want to be free. I want to break the hold of the enemy on my life. I put the cross of Jesus Christ between my heart and everything I was due to reap from the law of sowing and reaping. I give You permission, Holy

Spirit, to bring up whatever specific issues You want to bring up so that I can forgive specifically and repent specifically, because I choose mercy over judgment.

I tear up all those IOUs—all these records of outstanding debts—and throw them at the foot of the cross. I say that Your grace is sufficient for me. Whatever I loose on earth is loosed in heaven, and I loose it all into Your capable hands. I now give You, Lord, permission to work powerfully in my life, in Jesus' name. Amen.

Now, let me pray a prayer of authority and declaration over you:

Father, I take away the rights of the enemy over the lives of these people. Satan, I break your generational hold over God's people. I command you to loose them and let them go in the mighty name of Jesus Christ, God's holy Son. Free them, by the blood of Jesus that has never lost its power. I free you, woman of God. I free you, man of God. I free you, child of God. Mercy now triumphs over judgment.

I break off you all of those controlling fears, controlling anger, rejection and every hold of the enemy, in the name of Jesus Christ. I free you to rise to your full potential in Jesus Christ, your Savior and Lord. The Lion of the tribe of Judah has triumphed over all the power of the enemy. We put the enemy under our feet and step up into the grace of God, in Jesus' mighty and powerful name. Amen!

Study questions:

1. Why is holding on to hurts and judgments a luxury we can't afford?
2. What does the author mean by saying that we are on God's threshing floor?
3. How do we loose others through forgiveness?
4. Do you have IOUs—records of other people's debts to you—that you need to tear up?
5. Have you prayed the prayer? Are you willing to keep praying it until you see God's release in your life?

John Arnott, an international speaker and teacher, is well-known for his ministry of renewal.

His home is in Toronto, Ontario, Canada, where he attended Ontario Bible College. After graduation he pursued a varied and successful career in business. In 1980, while on a ministry trip to Indonesia, John responded to God's call on his life for full-time ministry.

He and his wife, Carol, planted their first church, Jubilee Christian Fellowship of Stratford, Ontario, in 1981. They started the Toronto Airport Christian Fellowship, where John is the senior pastor, in 1988. In addition, they have coordinated many new church plants.

John's ministry emphasizes God's "Father heart"—His life-changing love, grace, healing and deliverance. Since January 20, 1994, the Arnotts have invested much time and energy into imparting God's anointing to people in many different cities and nations. They are welcomed and appreciated wherever they go.

You may contact the Arnotts by writing to:

Toronto Airport Christian Fellowship
272 Attwell Drive
Toronto, ON
Canada, M9W 6M3

Phone: (416) 674-8463
Fax: (416) 674-8465
E-mail: ja@tacf.org